# Glass Kangaroo

Joe Pascoe

# Glass Kangaroo

## Acknowledgements

I wish to thank my wife Lyndel and our children Eve and John for all the joys of a beautiful home life. It is within the sounds and negotiated spaces of a busy house that the fire of love is kept alight.

I also thank Stephen Matthews OAM, Ginninderra Press, for publishing my work and for utilising his distinguished design sense to create such a fine book. I also appreciate the encouragement of the NDIS and Creative Art Therapy Australia in helping me realise my dreams.

*Glass Kangaroo*
ISBN 978 1 76109 583 2
Copyright © text Joe Pascoe 2023
Copyright © photographs John O'Neil 2023

First published 2023 by
**GINNINDERRA PRESS**
PO Box 3461 Port Adelaide 5015
www.ginninderrapress.com.au

# Contents

| | |
|---|---:|
| Preface | 9 |
| **1 Early times** | |
| Glass kangaroo | 13 |
| Shell lines | 14 |
| Bailed up | 15 |
| Leaving in the morning | 17 |
| Bushranger with a broken heart | 19 |
| Goodnight wee gun | 22 |
| Houdini the horse | 24 |
| Lake Dunn adventure | 25 |
| **2 Trying to think** | |
| Cliff before the sea | 29 |
| Wet greys | 30 |
| Strange box | 31 |
| Godot is waiting | 33 |
| On the bus | 34 |
| Bright mysteries | 36 |
| Scrapbook | 37 |
| Train chat | 38 |
| City train | 39 |
| Each to his own | 41 |
| Morning | 43 |
| Coming home | 44 |
| Space junk | 46 |
| **3 Encounters** | |
| Arthur Wellesley Arnold | 51 |
| The soldier | 57 |
| Anthony's hand | 59 |
| Johnnie's birthday | 61 |

| | |
|---|---:|
| Eve's dinner | 63 |
| Suits | 65 |
| I was surprised to hear my name called | 67 |
| Amor fati | 69 |
| Lost on a hill | 71 |
| Castlemaine visit | 73 |
| Looking for beauty | 75 |
| Unheard poem | 78 |
| An historian | 80 |
| And the kind therapist | 87 |
| Sweet kisses | 89 |

## 4 In nature

| | |
|---|---:|
| Nature's rain | 93 |
| Yarra dream | 94 |
| Dog Rocks | 97 |
| All waterfalls | 98 |
| In the park | 100 |
| On Dookie Hill | 102 |
| My friend the emu | 103 |
| Grass | 104 |
| Red bone | 106 |
| Chuchi and Lenny | 107 |
| Joseph Campbell and his eclipse | 108 |
| Rainy Carlton | 109 |
| Room 9 | 111 |
| Night kangaroo | 112 |

## 5 Stars

| | |
|---|---:|
| On the grass | 117 |
| Morgan's Beach sunset | 118 |
| Hanging moon | 120 |
| Piano and cicadas | 121 |

| | |
|---|---:|
| Don't go | 123 |
| Passed mothers | 124 |
| Rocky | 125 |
| Weeding | 129 |
| Christmas times | 130 |
| Alone like a shadow | 131 |
| Waves | 132 |
| The water | 133 |
| Australia | 135 |
| Black kangaroo | 137 |
| Grey then gone | 139 |
| Joe Pascoe | 141 |
| John O'Neil | 142 |

# Preface

Accidentally borrowing from Peter Carey's glass cathedral in *Oscar and Lucinda*, *Glass Kangaroo* is an imaginative symbol for recent Australia. Our kangaroo reappears some half-dozen times in different ways and times, across the 150 years gathered within this collection of poems.

The poems take us on a bumpy ride, encompassing landscape, law and order, jobs and the ongoing making of recent Australia. Both happy and sad, *Glass Kangaroo* seeks to reveal something of how everyday people make their lives in this magical land, and as also brilliantly caught in Carey's prose.

As a poet, I lack patience, but my impatience works if I stay balanced, skating fast on a thin ice of truth. Oh dear, what is truth? It's something you add to art, to make it spark.

Hide inside the land of the *Glass Kangaroo* and look with luck and love.

Joe Pascoe

# 1

# Early times

## Glass kangaroo

Glass kangaroo
Shattering the light
Every bound tearing the land apart

Baby joey in her pouch
Back streamlined for flight
With long hops
Your tail says goodbye

Furry kangaroo
Settled in the dusk
Three or four
Five even
Regal and passive
They look and decide
Relax they say
The sun is going away

Dark, dark now
Maybe gold with emerald eyes
Looking through me
I see them smile
You are good creatures
So well fitted into the land
Bushes bustling and crowding in
Night sky dropping
Those shoulders folding
Together in their camp
Warm and invisible
Glass kangaroos.

# Shell lines

for Lyndel Wischer

I dream with the shells
And their songs
Sound in my ears
Waves in my mind
Reminding me of ancient times

When land and sea were shared
Ghosts walked happily
Seeing their family
Joining in the dances
Smoke rises through the leaves
Blessing our midden

We are scattered now
Spirits blown through the land
Sweet songs curling around
Joining together again.

## Bailed up

It's their eyes
They sparkle, almost happy
A gun level with their heads

Then they fog over
Lose focus, widen
Go wet, then scan
Settling on fear and anger

It's a basic transaction
We watch and control
Get our job done
Move into their space
Reach into the pockets
Inside and out

Always a bit tough
We move together, avoiding crossfire
Ready to slap
Break them down

Our job done
Pinch their horses
Or cut them free
Keeping nasty

It's brutal, shocking
They will remember every little thing
Let them panic
Ready to piss
No fancy speeches from our lips

Our getaway is well planned
Diverse and confusing
Away from the ambush
Around the bend, we split up
Take long ways back
Vanishing where there is no track
The bush folding back

Their stagecoach will lumber on
Lighter, pretending to be brave
But personalities revealed
Spurious exclamations and announcements
The man turned into a woman
Women into men
Such is the humiliation

Brown-bearded coachman counts
No one shot, one fine watch stolen
Two brooches, three rings
They left the mail
Shook out the coins
Emptied the wallets
Not really much
A waste of time really
Mad fools
Soon for the rope
Captain Thunderbolt indeed!

# Leaving in the morning

I've seen those leaves before
Lazy in this foreign land
And those furrows
Like waves in the sand

Slowly with our horses
Such good company in these times
Together we will walk
Leather strap in hand

Dark clouds edging up
Pushed over the mountains
Ready to drop

A foolish wanted poster
Crushed in my pocket
Later we light a fire with it
And see our faces crumble

Warm blanket, meaty stew
Looking after you
You are a fool Captain Thunderbolt
Believing what you do

It's me, Mary Ann Bugg
That keeps a lookout
Thinking quicker than any gun
I keep the troopers guessing
We were never on the run

It's peaceful here
Brushed leaves making our bed
I felt your kiss on my head

Those stars above know our fate
I hear my ancestors say
'It's not too late'

On the morning dew
I will set the billy to boil
Whisper to my girls
'Creep back'

I'm sorry my love
You are no longer true
Thus I must say goodbye to you

Farewell Mr Ward
No ordinary man
But not so special that you can't die

It's time for our children
It's time for me too
And as you yourself often do
I bid farewell to you

Back through the leaves
We quickly disappear
Leaving you tea and flour
The horses know what I want
Off we go with a gentle trot.

# Bushranger with a broken heart

When something is not quite right
My horse sniffs
I count the bullets in my gun

One, two, three, four, more
Sit still on the saddle
Not too troubled

Lead me to the gate
Houdini my dear
Those cattle are mine
A horse too
Not as good as you

Men sweat when scared
Making their horses hard
I loosen off
Judging which way to go
Duffing is an art

Give me a cold moon
Smudge me gun with dirt
I'll not care
If someone gets hurt

I lost my heart at the circus
All stopped as he fell
It broke my simple heart

I loved people then
The children, dads and mums
Drunks and loons
Gasping, wanting tricks

The circus died
Its tent collapsed
What could I do?
Except juggle, do more tricks

Give me your money!
Open the gate
Don't make me late
I've got a date
A date tonight with fate

I dream of him
Now in the day
Going mad they say
Open, open heaven's pearly gate
Not for sheep you fool
But to see my beloved
Once more, dear sweet dream
Soon it will be another robbery
Bushranger that I am
Send a woman to make it grand
My tears run down to my hand
I raise the gun
Fire once, twice
Let the echoes ring out
No fear any more.

# Goodnight wee gun

Last shot fired
I don't need you any more
Those days are over
That past is gone
When you are in it
You can't see

I'll clean my guns
Keep my favourite
Sell the others down the track
Tidy and wrap my good one
The one that always felt right
Wrap it in an oily rag
Maybe bring it out sometimes
Spin the chamber
Cock the trigger
Let it click

No bullets anymore
Rattling in the draw
Just three kept near
Stored safe with my tea
In case I need thee

The noise is gone
Life is normal
No need to turn and squint
My baby is crying
My lads are all tall
Square and handsome
Like my husband of yore

It's time for believing
Helping and being
Living in the present
And seeing well ahead
Goodnight beautiful gun
It's time for you to rest
We lived longer than all the rest.

## Houdini the horse

Houdini is my name
I am a horse with a long mane
And a famous name
To escape and run
Is always a lot of fun
That's my game!

# Lake Dunn adventure

Our legend
Set within a dull dreaming
Endless, inflamed
We return

To look around
See our feet
On soil watched and worked
Silent now
Will the wind weep?

Our shoes are good
Cars parked, stopped
I walk away
Towards a quiet rise

It's a flute
Ready to play
Leaves shimmering
Flies buzz, lizards crawl
All old now

Our feelings are bracketed
It had to come to this
So far away
Now close, Lake Dunn
Wretched history
Men on horseback
Women at the homestead
Steady of mind
For years of heat

It was our dream
My brother and I
From a thousand miles south
We sat in classrooms
Tracing the map

First the Tropic of Capricorn
Then Rockhampton
Our childish fingers walking
Thinking, lingering
Ink stained

Our past
Deep within the land
We wondered all this
Six decades ago

Now we return
to where we have never been
To find
something we had never lost
To put together a puzzle
If only someone had spoken
To us little boys.

# 2

# Trying to think

# Cliff before the sea

Cliff before the sea
Calm before the storm
They say

Cliff before the storm
Sea behind the calm
You say

Itching at its base
Sand sweeping in
We need to talk

Your face looms
I try to swallow
Wrapping around you

You stand still
I have to move
Hot and cold

How can we meet?
In ease, crumbling together
Becoming rock pools of memories

Thus our love is shared
Through storms and rages
Calm and sweet on the sand

You and me, me and you
Together forever
Love in hand.

# Wet greys

A last day
Raindrops on the car
Enough to note
As they dance their tune
Adding melancholy to the beach scene

Picking up now
Making a walk unlikely
Blurring the windscreen
Water on water, the ocean greys
Dark rocks soften to smudges
Backed by white waves
Forming a flat pattern I guess

Less to report now
The rain is coming down
There is a green verge
Ahead of us, before the sand
Behind the old trees yawn
They have seen it before
They are not leaving
In and out, over and over
For all their lives
They will stay
A marriage of time and life.

# Strange box

Strange fruit
Lying in its box
Sloping forward
Its oddities in rows
Packed together for a long journey
Staring at me
On this Richmond footpath

Strange fruit
Black and charred
Seeing each other
As they died

Odd to think
Beyond belief
As a mother screams
Day and night

Strange boxes
Leaning into me
Can I choose?
Right or wrong
Pickled or smooth
Dark or light
Without taking flight?

I like the song
The ballad lets you in
Join in and sweetly sing
Remember your brothers
And try to hope
Lift yourself
And sing for the dead

Strange fruit
Strange fruit
I'll think of your home
I'll think of your beauty
Your long sleep
Eyes that can't weep
Hanging in rows
Pecked by the crows
Unexpected in the street.

# Godot is waiting

Garbage bin lids rattling
Becket calling
Using the theatre
In unspoken convention
Putting the rubbish in
Not out
For the audience to gasp
Not grasp
Our souls speaking?
They wonder
Plying for truth
Waiting for Godot.

# On the bus

He played his cards well
This old man on the bus
See you at 2 p.m.
Twice, for his wife, for clarity
To protect her
She was not alone
His wife

Two pensioners
Combined in the day's doings
Shopping and hydrotherapy
I learnt all this
The number nine bus
Well driven by its turbaned driver
Through Ballarat

Their love
Sure and still sweet
Spoken of between words
No edge, no swords
Held on pension day

Easy to speak
Wheels rolled
Useful informants
Where are the botanic gardens?
And Wendouree station?
Walkable, ten minutes
I gained much
A statement about a good shopping jeep
Special money, near neighbours, scripts
See you at 2 p.m.
He said, getting off
Open insurance for her
His wife of decades
As this stranger watches.

# Bright mysteries

Under a hat
Over a dune
In the twinkle of an eye
Old story, new story
Something in between
It follows you, you follow it
Sit down together
And share in it
For a bit

Tomorrow, the day after
And the day after that
Better get used to it
For it shall come back

You too can be a mystery
For someone to see
Remember to remember
To be kind and free
For it is the hope
That you find
And wisdom
Won't pass you by
As mysteries are made
To light life's parade.

# Scrapbook

Those bits and pieces
Torn and floating
Rough colours singing
Laughing like a collage

Rough piano playing
Refusing to worry
To how I feel about you
Funny mistakes
Commas and dots, stumbling sentences
I hope you get it anyway

My love for you
We get wild, you and me
And forget
Colourful storms, dried in the sun

On deck again
Warming
Someone is looking and smiling
It's you again
And me

Singing our collage
Our unstuck mosaic
Coming together, another topic
In our scrapbook.

# Train chat

for William and Kate Golding

Everyone is chatting
Train keeps on going
Mouths keep moving
I'm losing control

Station announcements
Mother calling her daughter
Detailed questions on the line

Quiet murmurs, voices played like cards
Emotional circuits
On this Sunday morning

It's all pleasant
But I feel annoyed
It's the recognition
Speaking English, speaking Australian
Everyday stuff
I feel I know it

My arrogance
Even an Asian with a shopping jeep
I'm too alert

The sky is darkening
It was sunshine
Maybe that will quieten down
My worthless complaint.

# City train

for Kate and William Golding

It's another train
Leaving the city this time
Warmed by its passengers
Less crowded, less busy

I'm relaxed now
It's my lack of vision
Sharpens my hearing
It cuts, but makes me defenceless

A quieter rattle
It's going through the old freight yard
I worked here once

A student amongst men
Tying things, a big Boy Scout camp
Outdoors, work to do
All men paid much the same
Roper, Slinger
Pride in the names

I like the railways
Always did
Toys, models, real
They all made me feel

Every sound connected to a purpose
Electric whines
Air con burbling
Brakes squealing
On it goes

We are a peaceful carriage, no chatting or talking for sport

A bit more rumble
Going through a tunnel
Under the city
Melbourne sitting above
Us sitting below
Just simply satisfied
Cosy, it smells well
City folk, deep in thought
Happy to go.

# Each to his own

In the train carriage
She sits there
I sit here
Voice overhead says
Arriving in Westgarth

He had a blue jumper
Neatly trimmed hair
I sit here
He sits there

Another lady
Two seats sort of
There is a balance thing
The carriage won't topple
Nor will we suddenly sing

Now arriving at Clifton Hill
Change here for Mernda
The announcer says

No chaos theory here
Molecules all lined up
Peacefully buzzing in a row
To the city we go

Friends and work mates
Artists and priests
Our children, our homes
Fitting together
Each mostly happy
Enjoying the pace
The place and how we must go.

# Morning

Sweet-sounding pedestrians
Birds in the tree
Morning it comes to all
It's a feeling of being free
Pity not the office workers
Warm enough in their coats
Daydreams filed away
Until the end of the day

Birds back to their nests
Armed with tiny twigs, plastic bits
Sharp in their beaks

We have got to hold it together
Wars and bushfires at bay
I don't want to say the word
But pray

There is always plenty of chaos
Letters tumbling, falling, crashing
Pick them up
Respect their place
Put them on the page.

# Coming home

Is that you, god?
Coming home
Living amongst men and women
How did you go?

Did they have space?
Let you into their homes
Or sleep out
In the snow, chilly autumn

You have gone four seasons
That time on the beach
Summer, I felt annoyed

Your first autumn, like now
It probably mellowed
In autumn people don't pray
But feel the earth
Everyone is a spirit
Joined

I find winter good for death
Your business, I know
Was it good, did you help?
Snipping their souls
Away from the body
Were you careful?
A noble task

Budding springtime
Weeds and flowers
Little lambs, birds in the morning
New birth
And death feels wrong

Thus it's turned to summer again
What did you learn, god?
Your handsome shape
Decisive, on the move
Are you less judgmental?
Found new ways to be wise
Dear god, can you share?
Powerful or not
Many of us still need a charm
One to hold in the palm
Safe in god's hand.

## Space junk

Antique antennae
Going by, still blinking
Pretty colours, odd shapes
Expensive and over-engineered

Lingering on
Lost dreams
Or dreams that were lost
It's the junk of hope
And jobs done!
Says a mind-reading relic

Such personalities, styles
A sense of something
Nostalgia, valuable
A museum goes by
Space junk!

It makes you think
Put it back together
Create a whirlpool
Or a tiny metal moon
Burnt out rockets
Wheels, wires, wobbly wings
Set to silent music
Orbiting in sequence
Dancing springs
Coiling on

Each with a history
Immune now to change
Give it a nudge
Watch it spin
Meaningless thing

A universe ahead
Progress by parts
Every gadget crafted
Something learned
Discarded now and for evermore.

# 3

# Encounters

# Arthur Wellesley Arnold

My name is Arthur
I clap my hands
And say my lines
To a lady at the front
The gentleman behind

Lean closer and I will tell you a story
A true one, not far from here
Perhaps you have heard of it
Indeed I know you have
Of blood, a flag and glory
Of ordinary men
And women too
Of a loyal dog
Tending its master, now still

That day in Ballarat
Etched in history
Big speeches, moral indignation
I was an actor too
That morning on Bakery Hill

You have heard of the Eureka Uprising
Its cause in licence fees
Shabby troopers, violent soldiers
And roaring fools
Fooling themselves
Revealing their souls
In speeches one, two, three

That was the moment
Everything was still
Words in the air
Air was free
And that's how the miners wanted it to be

Blue Jackets marched from Melbourne
Rough as guts was the road
In the young colony
Quickly sorting out the rebels
The government wanted its funds
To build better streets you see
To cart the takings from the goldfields
To their own Treasury

I carted the dead
Saw a man stuck like a pig
Pinned through like a bug
I was young and helpful
No weapons, except my personality
And a willingness to see god's day through

It was a trying few months
Sleeping tough and waiting
We miners believed in ourselves
Not in the Commissioner or Governor
With voices from around the world
It was fairness that the people wanted

We sit in a theatre tent today
Then it was a giant flag, flapping blue
Stars stitched on by the wives
Carried high, imagine if you will!
Now forever a mighty symbol
Seen every night in our sky
Felt in the warmth of our southern sun
A truth for everyone

I tell you
The demands were reasonable
Our weapons few
The day brewed
I arrived as a witness
Like an actor
To feel and be
A cypher be

Thirty men died
Filleted by shiny bayonets
Coursing red bloodying their white pants
Screaming 'Liberty!' as they drenched the dirt
Dirt turned to soil
Creating a new gold
A gold that could be shared
By all without a fee

What was it?
Free speech from California?
Famine from Ireland, Irish lucidity?
An awkward land?
Stony yet golden
Administrators working in British style?
All of those things and one more
The magic of Australia

Give us a chance
Reward our work
Jack is as good as his master
For a moment it had to be said
'We are free!'
That makes us all equal

The day had to end
An awful silence fell
But we were not surrendered
Nothing was forgotten
Bitter or sweet last breaths
Drawn and exhaled in finality
As history grew
I did too
Receiving a Green Ribbon fifty years later
Our claims for reforms gradually recognised
Those anxious miners driven to action
Humanity was the hero that noble day

Now I am married
And happily so
Linked on Bakery Hill
Digging in Avoca and Echuca
I hope they strike a nugget when they bury me
Shout the bar a beer and cry 'Liberty!'
So much history have I seen

My tale today is simple
In this canvas tent of life
Some men are very brave
But I am not one to be caught
Some men die via bayonet
But that was not for me
But instead I bred
A loving family
A dozen currency lads and lassies
That was my fate
My way of being free.

## Epilogue

Clap your hands as you leave this tent
This play, this theatre
Let it mean something to thee
Set your stride long
Help those you can
Look after this land
Hear the kookaburras cackle
Our new country saying hello
Now a Nation
Not for kings and queens
But for you and me.

# The soldier

Falling awake
Waking with loosened bones
Falling from sleep
Through the film
The film of feeling
Separating the worlds
Always the transition
Why the despair?
The grogginess I get
The war to get here
It's always muddy and difficult
Yet the descent is always a seduction
A wonderful slopping into cream
Then an adventure half-remembered
Enjoyed in its intensity
With colour and non-sound

And they dash together
As I ride
Or drop badly from my nap
A curious betrayal of feeling
Without meaning?

Rising from the ocean
To the whipping wind
To gather a towel
The sand so different from the water
The sand on the way in
Is felt slightly more on the way out
Under tender feet
Washed clean by the ambiguous ocean
Its questions understood by the swimmer
The idea of being wet is wetter than the idea
Overwhelming whilst reassuring
While the sand stays in view
Or out to the horizon seen in movement
Unattainable
Less important than the seabed
Reassuring, or fearful if not felt
Like a dream that is too deep
If you sleep too long

I cannot do anything but swim
And accept the sand
The purgatory of waking to the horror
My trench below Lone Pine
Which I had hoped to escape
Upon diving in.

# Anthony's hand

The past was here
when I shook his hand

Rough and tough
Some gentleness underneath

The years had stretch
Snapping back with a recollection

We know each other
So close over time

Ripped apart
Lives switching, so much pain

Useless periods
Did I say damage?

We reunite now
Old friends without history

Sometime later
Sometimes in between, missed

His hand hard
My hand soft
I shake with strength
His shake was easier

Swapping sides
Swapping tales

Joining once again
Circling like a clock

Tick tock
Tock tick
Him and me
Me and him
Even and honest
Sharing our half smiles
We have seen it before
In each other's eyes
And the way we walk
And talk

Neither of us knows.

# Johnnie's birthday

Edging on the accelerator
Little engine beating on
Steering lightly tensioned
Highway open, slipstreaming on

Then was then
Now is now
Looking for a signpost
Keeping on, keeping on

It's Johnnie's birthday today
I never could have forecast him
Strong and smart
A friend to his friends
Loyalty without loss
I like the way he plays

The sun through the windscreen
Sun on John's back
We all have to travel
Only sometimes turning back

We all give each other life
Life for life
Bubbling and floating
Free from too much doubt

Whatever advice I have for him
I might as well hear it myself
Something about enjoying a plan
Letting it ride, don't hide

It's a sunny morning
Nineteen years on
A full glorious day
The jacarandas will be purple in Sydney
Spreading across Summer Hill
Seen from the railway tracks
I rode home from the city
To see my beloved John again

Between then and now
There are 19 years tucked in
We went to the skate park
Monkey Puzzle toy shop
Visited the French patisserie
Rescued a gingerbread man
Always a life helping a life
That was the plan
Behold, a fabulous young man!

# Eve's dinner

Went to Upfield
Raining it was
Looked around
Umbrella up

Food shops
Cheek to cheek
Warm and friendly
Had to hold off
Dinner at my daughter's

Time filled in
Went back to the station
Fiddled some more
Went back three stops, still early

Listened to the radio
A man talking about being a sperm donor
Chances and fate
Things had caught up with him
Waiting now at Fawkner

It has to be said
The Fawkner Cemetery lacked ghosts
Keeping out of the rain?

Dinner was beautiful
Nutritious and delicious
Laughing together
Made two new friends
My daily quota

And so it was
It is what it is
Eve's new life
Flowers will grow
Lawns to mow, weeds ready to go
Hey, that's life.

## Suits

Suits
Two button, three
Pockets, shoulders, fabric
Hopes and chances
Honeymoon dances

Pants and jacket
They need shoes
To help them move

Hang them straight
Let them breathe
Handkerchief, keys
Wallet and phone
School diary, cigarettes
A sandwich in bits

Sackville grey
Hersch's the tailor
An opp shop
Myer
Henry Bucks
Peter Jackson
Fletcher Jones
Maybe twenty, if you really count

Looking for comfort
Style for a while
A uniform

They put people off
But let you in
Looking for a win?
Wear a suit.

# I was surprised to hear my name called

Hey, Bubble Bum!

This guy knows me
I thought
Primary school, some forgotten corner?

Reassuring in its way
The essential me
Pinned in the air

A simple phrase
Convincing
Without hubris, inverted pride
Sly and friendly
You can't escape the past

I say hello
Damien, Leon?
Names from then

Suburbs and schools ago
Marriages, mistakes
Are they in my eyes?

Health check, wealth check
30 seconds allocated
Where once it was days
He wants nothing
Just emotion
An easy smile, five minutes
Not my shoulder
Quick tilt
Of the head, not the pinball machine
No one even smokes
Not any more.

## *Amor fati*

Love your fate
The good gardener said
I felt surprised
Never heard that before
*Amor fati*

I'm surprised
A little refreshed
What a good idea

To be remembered
Hence this poem

Just in time
Might help with blood cancer
Should that actually happen
My good doctor hinted

Without much explanation
To be tested again
*Amor fati*
Sounds like a chocolate
A crooked smile

An ancient equation
Men in togas
Muttered quietly
While witnessing a misfortune
Preferably someone else's

It's an expression for old men
Cooling off from anger
Displacing regrets
And bad debts

My gardener is wise
So well read
Where do these modern philosophers come from?
I wonder

He is a mystery book
A strange shelf of knowledge
Self-taught by somebody
A seed was planted within
He grew and grew
Did Alex.

# Lost on a hill

Metaphor in the night

Connect two wires
Wind the handle
Watch it spark
Deep in the dark

I can't explain
Love's game

Knew it well
Felt its spell
Confused I'm on a hill
Soil, soil

Thoughts and feelings
Ideas gone mad
Does she love me?

Time may tell
Caught in a merry hell
Around and around
Flung, flung
Flying nowhere
Leery faces
Turn to stare

Can't think it through
Because of you
Tripping over
Standing up
Bad hiccups
Shaking me through
Eyes hurt
Metaphor blue
Trapped in a puzzle
Because of you

Need to walk
Try less talk
Let the sand settle
Sleep, sleep

Riddle, riddle.

# Castlemaine visit

Faint light in the room's high ceiling
Still there, decades on
Memories in the plaster

This old town
Golden gravel crunching underfoot
Rarely do you have to share the footpath

I like Castlemaine
A sullen bubble
Deflecting modernity
Organic cheeses in the supermarket
A warning sign to the rich

I come here to write poetry
Streets unfold like pages
Hills stall the view
Making you think anew

There, over there
That sound, near me
Touching crimped hedges
Watch for cars
It's pretty easy to do

Its layout awaits
I learn a bit more
Another section, another pub
Strange connections within
Making room, shifting

Tomorrow is Tuesday
A polite, blank canvas
Is this what a holiday is?

Time for a smile
Past 10 a.m.
Honest in my realism
A crow swears
Someone crunches past
Annoying cars travel by
Thongs flap on someone's feet
Still the light in my tall room weeps
It has no beat

Soft heart of Castlemaine
Murmuring beneath her streets
It's the leaves that tell time
Not the town hall
But do the church bells peel?
On a Sunday morn

Greeted by a Hot Rod
I had just left the art gallery
Eyed with mild suspicion
I eat

This town is quiet, secretive
Like an Italian walled city
It knows its golden worth
And sleeps without pity.

# Looking for beauty

It came in the sunshine
Again and again

Fine brown hair
Your moments dancing
We went there
You and me
Two small children
Grown trees

A long wave good-bye
Door closing
Wire grille rattling
Muffled footsteps
And your car is gone

It's mostly done
Mostly gone

Small residue on my mind
That was it
Drying in the sun

Feeling warm and cold
Mystery wrapped up
I guess I'm still alive

Love departed
Different to how it started
Once a fire
Not even a glow
Figuring which way to go.

# Unheard poem

Unheard poem
You're dying I hear
Unconscious and remote
A hole in your heart

You can't hear
Do you dream?
I think of you
See you standing
And talking happily
48 years ago

You became my brother's friend
A beautiful transaction
A coincidence
You and he travelled
Both great talkers
Both good walkers
Museums and galleries across Europe

For me you were a tutor
I was literally a poor student
I thought I was at art school
Not university, stoned
Some little wisdom came my way
Strange child that I was
Now I imagine you flat
Some pipes in
Some tubes out
A darkened room

Your hand touched at times
Loved for your spirit
As I liked you

This unheard poem
It's hard to end
It will write itself
With your quiet end
Goodbye Chris Wood

I hope the room is nice
There won't be a Caravaggio on the wall
Imagine that!
I hope you can

Perhaps you are walking down a cobbled street
Finding an ancient church
A small one with a great altar

*Madonna con Bambino* you exclaim
Wax tapers flicker
Casting shadows
Deep reds and superb blues
Heaven in your hand
Then out to the street
Into the light
Thoughts of saints mingling with dinner
Shared amongst travellers, new friends made.

# An historian

for Bob

Long pink fingertips
Peeling finely, dermatitis
An historian's problem
All that paper
Pages turned
Pages written
Gently patted flat
Right to left
Habitually smoothed out

A green, rounded rubber
An HB pencil
Sunlight through the window
A scene of serenity
Passions poured carefully
Adventures on the page
Quelled, vivid
In surprising balance

'As a child I made a filing cabinet
Rows of matchboxes
Glued together
And filed my postage stamps!

All those countries
Soft colours
Perforated edges
Postmarks proving their journeys'

Every paragraph a story
Or a contested debate
Invisible actors retelling history
To whomever will listen

Perhaps a purge, revolution
A king's head flopped
Blood in a basket
The queen screams
The people roar
Into the minds of the people
We must go

Scratch, scratch, scratch
Duck quill across the vellum
Tap, tap, tap
Keystrokes click
From simple sentences
To clever metaphor
History written, woven, painted

Choruses and melodies
Sometimes it is sung
Repeated or announced
Raw or rhyming
Repeated or strange
Our time understood

Plato kicked the poets out
Preferring research to dreams
Gathering in, not tricking
The historian is noble
The discourse essential
Livening the agora
Itself a brain
A university for all

Mind tempered by the heart
Whether by candlelight
By computer screen
Let it all be seen

An analysis of committee minutes
Decisions noted, quips unrecorded
Who was there?
Who was not?
Late night claret
Purple rings on the last page
A fascinating glimpse of a human stage

Fine artworks examined
Photographs to be considered
Puzzles in an old narrow street
Why is it here?
And not there?

'I taught my students to look
To find the ghosts
Faded signs of the past
And to analyse their glimpses'

The forgotten
The remembered
Their births and deaths
City names
Countries claims and maimed
And few left to weep

Swords held high
Children hide and creep
An unspoken bargain on the street
As chariots rolled by
They learned to hate

What was eaten?
And who stole what?
Dusty moral scales
A horse on the trot

Books as evidence
The writer's pen
Over and over again
Elegant prose
Reaching for a truth
To bewitch the reader, eager for a plot

Men telling lies
The dead silent
The rich and their many wives
Spies, eyes and wads of cash
Have I mentioned god yet?
He is worth a dash

The historian tells a story
She lectures well
Casting a spell
The art is in the delivery
Compressing so much
Into minutes and seconds
Whilst she has you
In her clasp

Back to the books
Seeing into mankind
Our mistakes, sweet efforts
He or she can't be too unkind
For find a person who has lived perfectly true
Always helped others
And built a fortune anew
To leave the world a better place
And I will show you
A humble one
Not always on view

'The lecture is over
The students listened well
They are from so many lands
In truth I feel under their spell

Their minds become pure
Perhaps recalling past lives
Not theirs but grandparents
I want them to birth new ideas
To bless their children with freedom and hope
History's greatest vision'

And of course, some footnotes:

1

Read Manning Clark
Our seer in an odd hat
Giving us a poem
A poetry to understand the land
Its gullies and twigs making us nimble
His modern bible about our land

2

Give me a good speech by Geoffrey Blainey
Casting about the room, eyes lifting us
Watch the slow bowling of history, he said
Understanding perfectly the aching nuance of the landscape
Trapping us, skilfully caught in his logic

3

It's Clare Wright that works a new spell
Taking us to Ballarat
An audio book too
History spoken
Blending voice and story to create a special place
Women's work, so memorable

4

Australian history can be hard to inhabit
That's our luck
Listen to Bruce Pascoe to understand why
Love the grass, he says
Be sensitive
Know the fish and the clouds, rain and fire
Seeds flying and dropping
Cracking in the embers
Gathered and scattered
Time, time beating with a low thump

Pray to the land
Graced by the winds
Flashed by the stars
Warmed by the yellow sun
Warming the red soil
Welcome the first peoples.

# And the kind therapist

for Robyn deVries

I see people
I create a calm atmosphere in the room
Soft brown cushions
A couch to sit and shift in
I try to be predictable to make it work
We need to work together
The small chat to start
Then a dip to an inner reality
On to the topic
Usually a close relationship
Gone wrong
Splintering love
I cannot argue
I listen fully
And focus
Steering subtly
My years of study inform
The primal nature of humans
In groups
In pairs
Alone
Tribes, families and marriages
They, him, her, need me
To find out
A way forward from their histories
I do not know how I do it
Oh yes, I know some theory

But of the other level
The rope bridge over the ravine
Swinging sickly
Gripping to step forward
Understanding the self
Your self
Your value
Find the good constructs
Linking the soul with the mind
If I may say
To make it to the other side
And enjoy the view
Of their life.

## Sweet kisses

Let my sweet kisses break your heart

Gathering you in in the dark
Push you quietly in the doorway
I won't tell you I love you
But it will spark

Feel me close
Trap you in
Make you surrender
And your knees bend

We are right
Each other
Know each other
Once old friends
Now lovers

Hold you quietly
Patiently
Hands in place
Embrace

Feeling you now
Clothes touching
Hands working
Telling our story
Small gestures flowing
Legs aligning
In that darkened doorway.

# 4

# In nature

# Nature's rain

I hold off
Words to the page
Let them litter, like leaves
Unselfconscious, easily passed over
Hardly felt in decent
Friends of the air
Then, plonk

Lying half flat
Colouring your steps, a path
Clues underfoot
Promising to return
Rusty and red
And green with grey
Brown on brown
Small moments
On a grand carpet

Cool under trees
Soft for your feet
Those leaves, gestural strokes
An alphabet of charming thoughts
Telling us to relax, to accept
Nature's rain.

## Yarra dream

Yarra River, talking to me
I don't know how
Upstream or downstream
Going on a walk, it follows
Keeping me company
Brown and mostly friendly

Oh, I leave it alone
Totally relaxed
Quite fat
Some shimmering eddies
Maybe it goes uphill in my mind
I'm not sure

But it talks
Polite, a casual hello
Then a reminder
Like, I am old
Simple stuff
A call to the trees
Their roots deep underground
So deep, curling under the river
Holding her in

My pathway is soft
Aqueduct level
Usually natural debris
Sung to by the birds
As meaningless to me as the bark on the trees
But coherent, full
Completing the scene

Its less brown way upstream
Diamond clean
Clogged and slow
At the bay
Coffee with sludge
Yet of the same cup
To be washed by rain
And filled again

Bends and curves
Loops and billabongs
Mile after mile
Hard to remember
Yet always recognisable
Ten rivers in one
But one broad mood

I have sat on your banks
Smoked a youthful cigarette
Kissed a young girl
Prickled my bum
I forget

You give to the rich
Give to the poor
Carry poems
Shore to shore
Cold in the shade
Cool in the middle
Yarra River, River Yarra

As I say
Left to right
Right to left
Glimpsed through trees
On a breeze
Gently tampered
Stopped and watched
You tell me to be thankful
And I obey.

# Dog Rocks

for Felicity and Peter Spear

I was born a long time back
Boulders on a gentle hill
A grey and jumbled puzzle under the Geelong sky
Seen from nearby, a curled fist
Remember, it says
A dozen smooth rocks
Crevices and gaps
Thrown and settled
Like a Zen garden, offering a quiet wisdom

Dog Rocks
Evocative, a primitive fertility at play
Thrown from the You Yangs?
An ancient volcano

My memory fades grey
Shiny in the night rain
I visit you again
Soft in the mind's eye
I still feel you
Alone.

# All waterfalls

Magic words forming in the waterfall
Water falling down
Dancing on the rocks
Skidding around

Looking up
Trying to see
Wet lips sprouting
Past an odd tree

Wait for how long?
Something beyond calculation
Vapour rising from the base
Freshening my face

I don't have to stare
Across the ravine
Bushes cling
Hoping to be seen

Round and round
Like a dream
Turning and turning
Counting, filling the stream

Sounding sincere
One note only
A wet orchestra
Playing one tune

Night time moon
Could, would I sleep?
Or just sit fazed?
Constantly amazed

Where would it take me?
Once it became dark
What would I remember?
Waterfalls in my past

It's so beautiful
White sound
Birds echoing
Car park forgotten
Foggy time rising
My tide receding
Flowing back

I give in
A little
Let it tug me
A wee leaf from that odd tree
Drifting free
Facing down
Ready to drown

But a shift, a flip
Floating like a ship!
One little leaf sails on
Troubles gone.

# In the park

Another day with Chuchi
Another walk, another talk
People and their pooches going by

Small nods
Skips and jumps
Sniffs and looks
That's what we all do

Two monstrous fluffy dogs
Pure white and clean
Real showstoppers
We stop and they gleam
So friendly, so perfect
Owned by a Japanese couple

They paraded on
We toured around
Covering a lot of ground
Ducks on the lake
Birds in the sky

Sunny day, regrets fallen away
My dog is taut on the lead
Right arm stretched
Following her
Chasing a bend

Adventure, loose stones
Puddles and claylike mud worlds
Grass green and close to her nose
I stay near, holding the lead dear

Days and days
Wearing a track
An easy pattern to repeat
Wear her out
Let her sleep

You begin to notice more
Work out her vocabulary
Judge my responses
Think it through
That's pretty much
What you do.

## On Dookie Hill

We went to Dookie
Saw the college
Dormitories in a row
Nicely done

Footy oval, neatly theodolited it seemed to me
An outdoor pool
A rectangle of perfect blue
And old roses too

Little roads
Maybe a toy town
Clever plantings
Heat and shade
Wheat and sheep
Dookie made the grade!

# My friend the emu

My friend the emu
Seen running
Happy, through the clearing
Old lady shopping
Get out of my way!

Not sure what to say
Hump of feathers on sticks
Pointy beak
Scrawny neck
I lay a big egg!

My friend the emu
Not sure she understands
I wanna hold your hand
Piss off young fella
I gotta stand

Hunting bugs
Running fast
Holding up the coat of arms
Don't get alarmed

Frightened of the bird
Peck your eyes out
Just beautiful to watch
Running free
Past that tree
Come with me
Dusty be.

# Grass

Types of grass
Seen from afar
Or just outside
Wet, dry
Soft and fluffy
Like fairy floss
Or short and sharp
Meandering weed
Looking to breed

Green as grass
Holding patches of dirt
Divots flying high
A golfer's curse
Putting green smooth
Nurtured and trimmed
Hallowed ground
Cricket pitch hard
Rolled up on the back of a truck
Some kind of luck

Saturday afternoon's noisy chore
Knowing galore
Beyond counting
Bonsai mean
Hardly seen
Nibbled clean
Goats gloating
What a scene

Placed in bins
Piled high
Haystacks!
Monet's painterly theme
Grass is not always just grass
If you see what I mean

Mix it up
Puff on a pipe
Inhale on a hookah
Watch it smoke
Singed by an ember
Or lie by a cool stream
And dream

That will do
Watch out for dog poo
Whipper-snipper near
Keep it under your feet
Until you are six feet deep.

## Red bone

Flick the bone
Red and plastic
Spinning in the air
Go, Chuchi, go

Caught in her eyes
Narrow shoulders back
Flexes her neck

Takes off
Which legs first?
Hard to tell
Something to do with her back
A torsion spring

Fast and sharper
Neat curve to the target
Tail flagging victory
Here, Chuchi, here!

# Chuchi and Lenny

for Luka and John

A sunny day
Chuchi and Lenny play
Two kelpies rounding each other

Sisters from birth
From Bundaberg
Collie coats
Blue Heeler spots

Quick through the bushes
Fast on the lawn
Chasing the prize

Getting older
Perfectly in tune
Both sit in a shadow at noon

They go exploring together
Like kids on bikes
Finding mysteries
Which they share

Bringing back our youth
Free of demons and care
We love you, Lenny and Chuchi
The way you dare.

# Joseph Campbell and his eclipse

The eclipse begins
The sun blinked
Mirror darkness
Birds stand still
Temperature drops
Feet disappear

I droop
My mind stills
Wishing for a superstition
And that kind of thing

It's good to change
Become a pagan for four minutes
Surrender to instincts
Ready to steal and scream

Looking around
Dusk to mini-dawn
Not much confusion
Traffic lights clicking on

A million miles away
A celestial body slides through
We spin and spiral too
A lonely blue marble in time and space.

# Rainy Carlton

Carlton on a rainy day
Lygon Street lights clicking
Who to remember first?
So many thoughts

Deep on a Saturday night
Fast made souvlakis
Tomatoes sliced like magic
And white yoghurt
At the Twins Café

Were there twins?
Certainly crowded at the counter
Cigarettes and Coke
Rolling around in my pocket
Rolling around with my friends
Alive in the fluoro light
Bright orange signs

Lights still clicking
Saturday afternoon
Putting Jacqui in the bin
Binning, Rodney called it
So innocent, so fun

Peter, Jacqui, Rodney
Names and games
Easy smiles

Lygon Street is still cool
Great food and movies
Nice black road in the rain
I'm happy to see it again

We went our separate ways
Not always sure where
Mother died near here
A difficult sadness
Gone from conversation
She liked the stories
Tales of my friends
Her 95 years finished in Carlton
Lucky her.

# Room 9

Little beautiful sunset
Framed by my window
Overlooking Castlemaine
Room 9, Campbell Street Lodge

Hanging there
Plasma screen perfect
Unexpected and neat
Flinty iron rooves shine back

Smooth colours
Really only two
Feisty yellow
Moorish blue

Quiet across the valley
A whole township
Do they get this every night?
This fine view
Through curtains, over gardens
Room 9 please
I like the view.

# Night kangaroo

Glass kangaroo
Now resting in the moonlight
Clouds passing over
A deep blue here and now
Crouched in the vague shadows
Easily forgotten
Even by the observant

We pass
You stay still
I sniff
Still nothing
Forgetting quickly

Towards the beach
Hoping to hear the waves
Does she go to the beach?
Hop over the sands
I've never seen her prints

Back from my swim
Feeling natural
Walking back
Nothing to be seen
But so much to feel
I'm blending in
No longer listening
Just vaguely avoiding tripping
Feet gliding in the dark
Finding the path
Knees softly bending
Like a kangaroo.

# 5

# Stars

# On the grass

Glass kangaroo sleeping
Stars shining through
Warm bodies touching
Grass easing flat

Paws curled
Natural and perfect
Like carved wood
Makes you wonder

Tail in place
Between you and her
Tiny joey safe
Sniffing as she sleeps
Ears resting, antenna down

At peace
Settled
Just a group
In the dark
We all settle
In our groups
During the night
Stars lighting our dreams
Feeling the warmth
Feeling our family
Soft grass springing
Breathing so quietly
Curling around
Until dawn's sunshine arrives
Shaking the dew
Making the green grass easy to chew.

## Morgan's Beach sunset

Sunset stretched out over low tide
Cool on the toes, sand wet
No hurry and well timed
We walked there through the bush
Itself a fairy cave
Fine petals, softened middens
Still someone's place

The track curved and swayed
Around bigger trees, here and there
Private and enclosed
A ribbon shaken loose
Falling easily on the ground
Matching our steps

It wavered a little near to the sand dunes
Philip and Lyndel playfully tumbled to the beach
We all kicked off our shoes
A sweet communal pile
A family marking its spot
No real rules as Daisy took off
Running as she wished
Paws kicking tracks

We ambled and talked to the edge
A shifting border
Clean water sliding in
Reaching back to the setting sun
It was bright yellow
The sky was a perfect blue
The dunes were olive capped with scrub
But the sound!
It was tonal and washing our souls

Three and two and one
Lachie counted down
The sun sank
Flattening the horizon with a huge smile
It remains light
My own son John, brown and strong
We turned after a while
Not transformed, still the same
Close on Morgan's Beach.

# Hanging moon

Glowing brooch
On the breast of the heavens
Dark skinned beauty caring for us all
The brooch slips between breasts
As she leans over us
To protect
To love
We sleep on
Safe in our dreams
Pearl swings
Bright and dull at times
Shrouded and naked in lace
Unblinking
Deep and far away
Giving us light
Almost enough to read by
Seeing the plants breathe
As they grow
Stepping onto the friendly path
Behind my house
Which we own
Mortgaged in love
All feels good
With gentle excitement
I stalk the shadows
Feeling the primitive strength
For a pleasant while
To slip back inside
To bed.

## Piano and cicadas

for Gabbi Alberti

Piano and cicadas
Playing together
Promising to be hot
Both quick on the tempo

The bugs pause
Gathering a breath
Back on
Continuous

Stopped now
I can listen in
To the piano
Debussy on the radio
All quiet in the soil outside

The playing has beautiful pauses
It's a very fine piano
Think of its blackness
Gently played

Night time tiring
Stars yawning
A long day gone
It's complicated, stuttering on
Like the piano
Like the cicada

My legs soften
Shoulders too
The piano marches
Working away
Irregular within its pattern
Like the cicadas
Intense and fast
Double counting
Back and forth
Words gone.

## Don't go

Come back, don't go
Not yet, don't go
She said
From behind her plaque

A warm day at the cemetery
Bindies caught in my socks
Tall weeds took on a graceful air
Like thistles, irregular
The graves did their job
Only slowly shifting in the heat

It's a charming scene
Sweeping gently
An ancient sand dune
Somehow under inland Shepparton
But that's Australia

Beyond time
Such a great land
But I digress
Her voice was gentle
Clear and singular
Don't leave
But I turned
Laying a hand-kiss
On the cool brass
Read the names of her children
Elizabeth, Robert and Joseph.

# Passed mothers

For the motherless on Mother's Day
You remembered
I know

Did you pretend to ring?
Like you may have
Or felt too close
I know I did

Once in a while it felt easy
But it could feel too much
I know

Did she mind the absences?
When a child leaves home
Goes to university
Changes class
Has a snobby girlfriend
I know

She is dead now
Long cold
Sealed
Ash

What more?
Not much
But memories remain, distilled

Happy dead Mother's Day
It's a thing
You know.

# Rocky

It's got heat
And a river
Great steaks they say
When the rodeo is in town

I remember it's green
Almost violent in the sun
Walk on the shady side
To get your chores done

Mount Archer, Fitzroy River
East to Yeppoon and out west
A long drive to where you want to go

There are towns with their names
Aramac, Emerald, Jericho
Lake Galilee, Lake Dunn
Where two half-brothers became undone

Ghosts on horseback
Camp dogs snore at night
Flies rest as the moon rides
History slowly shifts
Even as we resist
A hard land, if you fight

Some shops here and rare
Tin balconies cutting the glare
Creaking doors letting you in
Maybe its milk
Softened with a quiet grin

How you own this country shows
A light loose stride
Not put on
Keeping people wide
Something that rhymes is glide

People will tell you a story
An uncle may open up
I got married there
My dear first wife Dolly
Her funeral too

This landscape has a map of sorts
A game played across time
As the Aboriginals will tell you
Those lumps and bumps mean something
That washed sky
Those days when it all breaks
And starts again

Rockhampton's streets are well laid out
A big Customs House
Designed with purpose, no doubt

It's a place that sticks on the map
You can't really drive around it
I can't think of a reason
See it from Mount Archer, looking back

We dreamt of it as children
Bobby and I, far south
It filled our imaginations
As our father sailed away
Tough, we didn't cry

A myth for us
One of our very own
I'll use the word stone
Because it rhymes with mother alone.

# Weeding

Making the garden
Weeding left to right
Small grass
Grasp it
Drop to the path
Move along
And back and forth
A circular motion
Leaning over, determined

My mind focused
Whole muscle groups clench
And look around
Admire and critique
Those small shoots
Are they weeds?
Or once plucked, correctly restored

It's just a square metre
Our garden is terraced
A handy arrangement
Promising a picture
Flat rosemary with tiny blue flowers
I put it there
Resonating with the grass tree
And so it goes
No plant is alone
Sharing its soil with another
Another and together
That's what makes it a garden.

## Christmas times

Magic in the air
It's Christmas in two days' time
I give it a chance
Let it breathe through me

Some belief is good
Just let it run
A spirit circling the paddock
That flows, cooling the grass

I let it come
Just once a year
We all need it
To show humility, a way of being fair

It slides on
A few natural days
Savouring the light
Soft blue agapanthus
They sway just a bit
Putting the year to bed

A year stops
It pauses, holds still
We join together
We hope, we kiss
New minutes soon arrive
I look around
People in the dark
Feeling as one.

## Alone like a shadow

Alone like a shadow
Deepening until gone

So hard to believe
She's really gone
All the time
So hard to believe
Feels like a crime

Alone like a shadow
Deepening until gone

Your words and mine
Gone is the feeling
No love on the line

Alone like a shadow
Deepening until gone.

## Waves

The ground has been shifting underneath
I have learnt to surf
High waves ready to dump

Breathe in the water
See the sunlight
Breaking in from above

There is beauty there
I feel nothing
Cold from the cold

Remembering my task
Float to the top
Always land in sight

Rest in the swell
Break the spell
Swim free.

## The water

Most of the time
When crossing roads
And saying hello

When meeting others
And staying on time
I care most of the time

Other stuff can slip
My kids don't need my trip
Most of the time

I can run but mostly I look
Booze is gone, dope too
Respecting what, believing no

Devil taped me once
Jesus is not my crew
But listen, brother
That's what to do

In between
Or on top
It won't stop

Life is a stream
Pebbles underneath
Sky overhead

Stay in the water
Let it help you
That's what to do

Feeling this beer
River banks brew
Old grey bushes
Loving those leaves

Floating, floating
Murray River, Goulburn too
Singing, humming for you

Smoothing it down
This won't stop
This loving of you.

# Australia

Australia
Who are you?
A brown autumn leaf in Melbourne
Cold water off Hobart
Heat in Lichfield National Park
Nude beach, crocodile squint

Lady in a doorway
Man dying in a hospital
Children peddling plastic trikes

Cop in a leather jacket
Kind dogs, proud cats
TVs, mobile phones
And a train hoots

We are not sure
Our leaders are OK
Mostly trying to sway us
Still the great conversation
Still a big paddock

I cannot see it all
Though I have been in many kitchens
Made some money
And spent it too

A glass kangaroo
Through which we view
So much on view
Impossible yet probable
You carry us on your back

Bounding through time
Hopping over fences
Protecting your young
Ready to fight anyone

I still don't get it
Why we don't leap higher and longer
And look further ahead

We are that glass kangaroo
Fragile and strange
Belonging to all
Sold out for small change

Be brave
Be wise
Stick together
Look for the dewy sunrise
Birds will call
Bumps and noises all around
Our feet on the ground
Fly in the sky
One walking on my nose!
Swot it away
Look forward every day.

## Black kangaroo

Black kangaroo
Hopping through
Such swag

Shiny boots, white teeth
Punchy punk
Try me
See what happens to you

Black kangaroo
Smarter than you
Ready to do you

I'm Mohammad Ali
Charlie Perkins
And a kid you don't know
Yet!

Future girl, future boy
Woman, man
Look into my eyes
What do you see?
Deep anger
Sweet hope
The old people
Children to come
All there in a black kangaroo

I'm going somewhere, without you
Finding my mob
Calling out, little snickers
Chewing, smiling

Not you
You are not me
That's it
Believe it, it's true

Maybe wait
Sunset, sunrise
Then maybe we can be one
Not the same but one

I'm not sure
Time helps everyone
Can I help you?
Maybe, maybe
Let's see what we can do
This black kangaroo.

# Grey then gone

So young, bouncing away
Fine grey
Already offering camouflage
Like a bush on the move
Just happier

A feminine face
Kind eyes alert
Ears very pert
No slouching here

A few serious looks
She or he changes direction
A gear change
Big feet, thumping tail
Over and gone
We are left to admire

A job to be done
Let's hope for fun
Turning a picture book
Opening a page
Old kangaroo now
Wise and sage

Special from birth
How many hops in a year?
Becoming invisible
Showing no fear

Almost done
Sound soft
Great life fading
Rest now
Peaceful in the dust

Still, still
Last eyes looking
Turning to glass
Going fast
Shattering glass

Not much more
Yet more there is
Our thoughts linger
Memories fight with feelings
A thousand pieces scatter
You helped us to see
Glass kangaroo.

# Joe Pascoe

Joe Pascoe has published several poetry books with Reading Sideways Press, including *Gum Tree Burning*, *Frangipani* and *Sharp Pencil*. Joe lives in Ivanhoe, near Melbourne. In this collaboration, he is seeking to present a large metaphor for life and adventures in Australia, both new and old.

# John O'Neil

John O'Neil is a nationally regarded Australian photographer represented in such collections as Deakin University, Geelong Art Gallery and the National Gallery of Victoria. The photographs in *Glass Kangaroo* were mainly taken near Torquay, Victoria, where John has lived for many years. John sees the kangaroo as a symbol of love, providing continuity over millennia.

www.ingramcontent.com/pod-product-compliance
Lightning Source LLC
Chambersburg PA
CBHW071504080526
44587CB00014B/2205